Journaling

Access What's Within;
It Awaits You

Pat Heydlauff

Other Books by Pat Heydlauff
Conversations with Thoth: Your Pathway to Wisdom, Truth, and Unconditional Love
Looking Within: Discover 7 Principles Leading to Hope, Peace, and Joy
Feng Shui So Easy a Child Can Do It
Selling Your Home with a Competitive Edge
21 Ways…to Increase Employee Engagement
The Way We Go: Your Roadmap to a Better Future

Welcome

During my quiet time with pen and paper is when I tap into my deep spiritual connection and find messages within. This is known as Creative Journaling.

Creative journaling is not the same as tracking daily activities or keeping a diary. Creative journaling requires that you quiet your mind and listen for the message being given to your heart from your guides, angels, or your Creator. You know it's the truth when the message you hear is in your best interest, serves a higher good, and brings no harm to others.

For me, journaling is a two-way street of 24/7 communication and connection. It acts like meditation or prayer. I ask questions, and I get answers, or I get what is standing in the way of the answer. There have been times in the beginning when I've had to take care of several "somethings" standing in my way before I got the answer to the question I originally asked; but the answer always comes.

There are at least four types of Creative Journaling.

1. **Accessing Information Within Journaling** can take the form of spiritual growth, seeking wisdom and knowledge within, consciousness, or transformation. Make every day count! Realize that whatever you do today, you are exchanging for a day of your life. When journaling, you are choosing to learn, grow, and succeed.

2. **Gratitude Journaling** allows you to acknowledge all the good in your life. It provides you inspiration and encouragement. The more grateful you are for everything in your life, the less time you have to feel sorry for yourself. You'll soon realize that a lot more things have gone your way than you thought.

3. **Dream Journaling** happens after you've had a vivid dream and you feel there is a message you need to remember. Keep your dream journal by your bedside so you can record your dream immediately upon awakening. Dreams are often messages filled with answers to questions, inspiration, encouragement, and even warnings.

4. **Manifestation Journaling** is a way of expressing your needs, wants, and goals to your spiritual guides and Creator. By writing what you want down, you give clarity to your objective and provide it energy to

grow. In some ways it is a little like the law of attraction. What you focus on comes to you. My favorite time to write manifestations is every month as the new moon arrives. Be as specific as possible with a time frame involved.

Some people like to do all four types in one journal, but I prefer to have separate journals for Gratitude and Dreams. They can be quite long and deep, so they often deserve their own book. By using separate journals for the specific areas, you can easily look back to see what dream you wish to recall or what you were grateful for on a specific date. You can also enjoy seeing your growth.

Now, let's get started with your creative journaling.

Quiet your mind so you can hear. Close your eyes so you can see. Since you receive information through all your senses, they must be completely void of everything so you can bring the new information into your physical being.

1. Get into a non-distracting quiet space.
2. Quiet your mind; close your eyes.
3. Focus; keep your mind free of thoughts or empty so new thoughts can enter.
4. Look and listen to discover what is hiding behind the veil when you are in quiet solitude.
5. With closed eyes and an empty mind (quiet music for some), you will see and hear truth, love, and light. Write what you hear, feel, or sense.
6. Be sure to date each journal entry so you can review your progress months or years later. Keep your journal in a private and safe space where no one else can read and misinterpret your words of seeking and wisdom acquired.

While I can journal almost anywhere, I usually journal in my studio, which is dedicated to creativity, in my case, painting and writing. I eagerly look forward to every morning to begin my journaling and my adventure for the day.

Once you start journaling, you can never really stop. It will be only a matter of time before you will return to it. I feel so connected when journaling that I long for it when I stop for any length of time.

This is where your story begins. May you find wisdom and knowledge as you unload negative things holding your back. May you find truth and blessings as you begin your journey.

-Pat

We Are Becoming Us

The time for awakening is here.

The Divine is by our side.

There is no fear of failure.

The words will flow, the knowing comes,

and the being is.

✵✵✵✵✵

Looking Within, page 45

Date: ______________________

Date: ______________________

Date: _______________________

Date: _______________________

Date: ___________________________

Date: ___________________________

Date: ___________________________

Date: _______________________________

Notes

Date: _______________________

Look Within

Look within to find all answers

Look within to see what you seek

Look within to align the human with the spiritual

Look within to create your wealth

Look within to become who you are.

★★★★★

Looking Within, page 61

Date: _______________________________

Date: _______________________

Notes

Date: ___________________________

Notes

Date: ________________________

Date: ___________________________

Notes

Date: _______________________

Notes

Date: _______________________

Date: _______________________

<table><tr><td>

Notes

</td><td>

</td></tr></table>

Date: ________________________

Take Control

Take control of your life

so it becomes what you choose.

Take control of your life

put aside the unimportant.

Take control of your life

put aside the unnecessary.

Take control of your life

put aside others.

Take control of your life

put aside Earth thinking.

Take control of your life

put aside the human ego.

*****

Looking Within, page 75

Date: _______________________

Notes

Date: _______________________

Notes

Date: ______________________________

Date: ______________________________

Notes

Date: ___________________________

Date: ________________________

Date: _______________________________

Date: _______________________

Notes

Date: _________________________

With true wisdom, the mind disappears and you become one with the all-powerful energy of the universe, the Divine, the Great Spirit, First Source, the One.

✮✮✮✮✮

Looking Within, page 98

Notes

Date: _______________________

Date: ______________________

Notes

Date: ___________________________

Notes

Date: __________________________

Date: _______________________

Notes

Date: ______________________

Date: _______________________

Connect With God and the Universe

Connect to the power within so your thoughts can be

received with clarity.

Connect to the power within so you can create the

future you choose.

Connect to the power within so you can overcome

anything standing in your way.

Connect to the power within so you can honor all.

Connect to the power within so you can maintain your

spiritual continuity.

Connect to the power within so you can find hope,

peace, and joy.

✶✶✶✶✶

Looking Within, page 123

<u>Notes</u>

Date: _______________________

Date: ______________________

Notes

Date: _______________________

Notes

Date: ___________________________

Notes

Date: ___________________________

Notes

Date: ___________________________

Date: _______________________

Date: _______________________________

Date: _______________________

Listen for the still voice within and you will always hear.

Listen for the still voice within and you will know.

Listen for the still voice within and you will be wise.

Listen for the still voice within and you will hear the truth.

Listen for the still voice within and equality will become reality.

Time is truth. It is now.

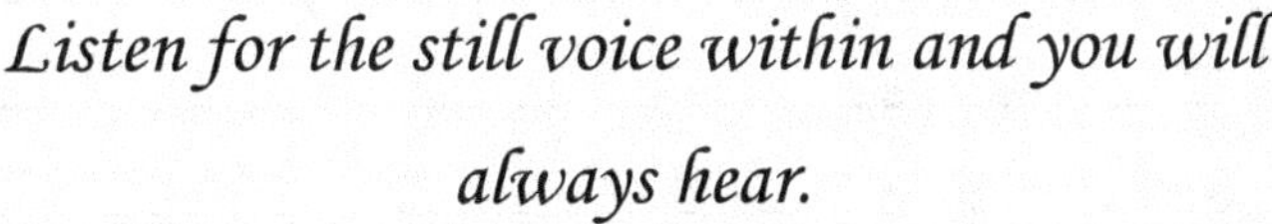

✮✮✮✮✮

Looking Within, page 148

Date: ______________________________

Date: ___________________________

Date: _______________________

Notes

Date: _______________________

Notes

Date: ______________________

Date: _______________________

Date: _______________________

Notes

Date: _______________________

Date: _______________________

Eternal Access

When you access your heart,

You find your voice within

When you find your voice within,

You discover your path

When you travel down your path,

You become connected to God and the universe

Once you are connected to God and the universe

You find PEACE!

★★★★★

Looking Within, page 197

Date: _______________________

Date: _______________________

Notes

Notes

Date: ___________________________

Date: _______________________

Date: ___________________________

Date: _______________________

Date: _______________________________

Date: ______________________________

Date: ______________________________

Take Time

Take time to breathe, you have much to do.

Take time to rest, you need to ration your energy.

Take time to be, you must live in the moment.

Take time to listen, the messages are always available.

Take time to reflect, you will tap into the eternal

information.

Take time to connect, the universe awaits your arrival.

Take time to create, you will reach your destiny.

Take time to find joy, it makes your heart smile.

Take time to love yourself and others, you will find

peace.

★★★★★

Looking Within, page 207

Date: ___________________________

Notes

Date: ___________________________

Date: _____________________________

Date: _______________________

Notes

Date: _______________________

Date: ________________________

Notes

Date: _______________________

Date: _______________________

Notes

Date: _______________________

Do You Know

Do you know, it is your turn

Do you know, it is your turn to unveil you

Do you know, you are connected

Do you know, the universe and others await

Do you know, you are important

because you are you?

★★★★★

Looking Within, page 214